Cuba

Experiments in Tourism and Development

Babu George

Thomas Panko

Preface

Cuba has long been a popular destination for American tourists. Due to Prohibition in the 1920s, Cuba became an attractive escape destination for many Americans. American tourists did not harbor animus toward Cuba even during the bitterest days in U.S.-Cuba relations. The political taint simply caused Americans to view Cuba as "forbidden fruit." As of this writing, American policy towards Cuba is in flux. After a short stint of friendliness during the presidency of Obama, there is anxiety about how the new administration will deal with Cuba. President Donald Trump (2017-) is yet to take a definitive stance, but his interim directives have made travel to Cuba more difficult.

It is not often that hopes shape tourism development. However, there is widespread hope about the future of tourism in Cuba. Many multinational hotel developers have expressed interest in investing in the hospitality sector. Currently, Cuba does not have an adequate tourism-focused infrastructure to support additional tourists, even during off-peak seasons. Professionalism in the industry is yet to be developed and matured; it is in a state of flux. When a small cruise ship brings a couple of hundred visitors, coastal cities are overwhelmed. Notwithstanding, the Cuban authorities are presumptuous about their ability to handle any number of additional visitors. If American tourism to Cuba increases, it will be no easy task to provide them with the requisite facilities.

Other Caribbean island nations are cautiously assessing how relaxing the U.S. embargo on Cuba would affect them. Many of these countries were beneficiaries of the embargo. It is not evident whether they have plans to deal with Cuba's re-emergence into the tourism map. Some experts, however, aver that there are enough tourists to meet the targets set for the Caribbean and Cuba won't be hurting the overall tourism demand for the Caribbean.

There are perplexing signals coming from Cuba. With the Venezuelan crisis, gasoline is already being rationed in Cuba. The Cuban economy fell overall in 2016, despite a significant hike in tourism-related revenue. Cuba cannot import even the most essential commodities due to its quickly depleting foreign exchange reserves. Tourism might offer the swiftest way to replenish foreign exchange. But, Cuban authorities are taking a cautious approach, especially given the socio-cultural and environmental impacts of unleashing tourism. That said, there is also a heightened realization that the country cannot continue to survive on subsidies from foreign governments.

This is not a formal scholarly treatise and personal opinions are proffered. However, given the paucity of scholarly research on tourism in Cuba, it is hoped this effort will serve as a launchpad for other serious minded researchers.

Acknowledgements

We acknowledge the insights of numerous Cubans – both laymen and the scholarly minded ones, that went into the ideas presented in this book. We have had extensive consultations with several Cuba experts. Particularly, we acknowledge the contribution by Dr. Tony Henthorne, Professor of Tourism at the University of Nevada Las Vegas and one of the world renowned Cuban tourism experts. He gave us a patient hearing in answering some of our questions. Ms. Chelsie Andrews, the graduate assistant of the first author assisted with some literature review that went into the final chapter of this book. In general, we thank all our friends and family who cooperated with us and encouraged us during this project.

Contents

Chapter 1

A Passage Through the Early History of Cuba

Looking back, Cuba was home to a number of Mesoamerican cultures prior to Columbus discovering the island. Cuba's pre-Columbian history dates back to somewhere around BC 4000. The ancient site of Levisa had developed into a settlement dating from approximately 3100 BC. The Cayo Redondo and Guayabo Blanco Neolithic cultures flourished between BC 2000 – BC 1000 in western Cuba. In many instances, an existing migrant group would be driven away by a new wave of immigrants. For example, the indigenous Guanajatabey inhabited Cuba for centuries, but were driven away by Taíno and Ciboney migrants. The Taínos population reached nearly 400,000 by the time of the Spanish invasion. The Taíno, likewise, had become very successful in agricultural activities by the 15th century. They cultivated large amounts of yuka roots, sweet potatoes, maze, tobacco, and cotton. The geographic location of Cuba is given in Figure 1.1.

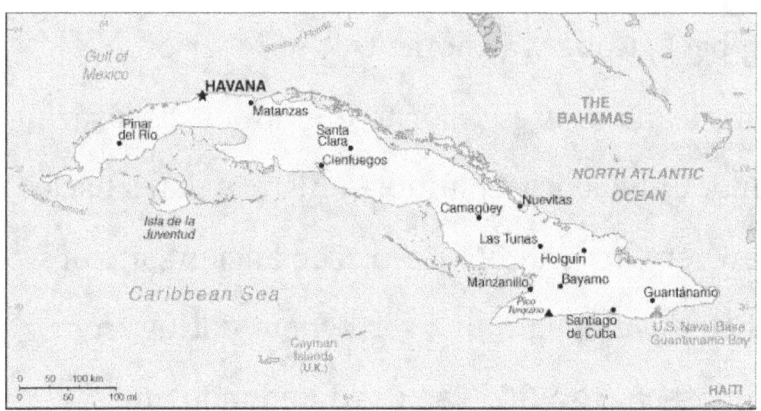

Figure 1.1 Map of Cuba showing its geographical location

The history of Cuba's relations with the rest of the world began with the arrival of Christopher Columbus in 1492. Columbus strayed off course on his planned Spanish-sponsored voyage to India and thought Cuba was a tip of the Indian peninsula. In fact, Hispaniola (present-day Haiti and the Dominican Republic) was discovered slightly before Cuba and became its first settlement. During his first voyage,

Columbus landed at the northeast coast of Cuba. He made a second voyage in 1494. During that voyage, his ships passed along the southern coast of the island and he explored various inlets. Columbus seemed to have been fascinated with the tent-like homes made of palm leaves in which the inhabitants lived.

Soon after the first voyage of Colombus, Pope Alexander VI decreed that the Spaniards were morally bound to convert the pagans of the New World. This sanction was a great booster for subsequent European conquests and colonization. Spanish atrocities were interpreted as much needed punishments to evict the evil spirits who occupied the bodies of the pagans and mass murders were justified as the defeat of the devil. The Spanish invasion culminated in the nearly total elimination of the aboriginals. Many others died from communicable diseases. These acts may have served as the first known absolution in history.

Encomienda, the order from the Spanish Emperor that the conquered people be considered vassals of

Spain and their services be used as a reward for the conquerors, established a formalized legal system in the Americas for the first time in history. At the same time, it made the life of the remaining natives a perpetual misery. There were several versions of encomienda implemented in Spanish colonies. The abuse of native people under the encomienda system made it very controversial, and some priests working in the colonies kept pressuring the Crown to rescind the practice. Finally, the crown-managed repartimiento system replaced encomienda throughout Spanish America. Some provisions in this new system incentivized natives for disowning their tribal identities, resulting in a proliferation of marriages between natives and Spaniards.

It took nearly fifteen years before the entire Cuban coast was mapped; early Spanish settlements were established about the same time. In 1508, Sebastián de Ocampo, a Spanish navigator and explorer, circumnavigated the island under the authority of the

Governor of Hispaniola. He sailed against the Gulf Stream, the voyage taking about eight months. Ocampo's effort removed any doubt that Cuba was a peninsula.

Spanish settlements on Hispaniola and the Cuban islands grew quickly. The tribes did not provide a "red carpet' welcome for the new settlers; guerilla warfare lasted several years and ended with the capture of chieftains who were then burned alive. Even in instances when the invaders were welcomed, the consequences were the same for the natives. According to the Spanish friar cum historian Bartolomé de Las Casas, more than three thousand locals were butchered in Manzanillo by the colonizers, without any provocation. Actually, the locals were waiting to greet the Spanish with bread loaves, fish, and other food items. Even those who escaped to the mountains and smaller islets were later captured and killed. A few fortunate ones were confined to reservations.

Chief Hatuey from Hispanola led the natives against the Spaniards and became one of the first fighters against European colonialism in the New World. He and his men had fled to Baracoa in Cuba as a result of the Spanish exploitation of Hispanola. His team along with a few native Cubans, made preparations for an expected Spanish onslaught of Cuba. Apparently, most of the Cuban natives did not take his words seriously. When Spanish forces finally marched into Cuba, Hatuey fought back employing guerilla warfare. The following famous speech is attributed to him:

"Here is the God the Spaniards worship. For these they fight and kill; for these they persecute us and that is why we must throw them into the sea. They tell us, these tyrants, that they adore a God of peace and equality, and yet they usurp our land and make us their slaves. They speak to us of an immortal soul and of their eternal rewards and punishments, and yet they rob our belongings, seduce our women, violate our daughters. Incapable of matching us in valor, these cowards cover themselves with iron that our weapons cannot break."[1]

Using less than stellar means, the Spaniards captured Hatuey. He was tied to a pole and burned alive in 1512. Just prior to the execution, he was asked by a priest who was present if he would accept Jesus in order to avert hell. He replied that he would not want to live in heaven if it was with the Spanish oppressors. His is lovingly remembered by many as Cuba's First National Hero. An old painting depicting slave labor is given in Figure 1.2.

---

[1] Bartolomé de Las Casas, Short Account of the Destruction of the Indies. Translated by Nigel Griffin. (London: Penguin, 1999) ISBN 0-14-044562-5

Fig 1.2 Slaves unloading shipments, commanded by their black masters

Hispaniola was slowly replaced by Cuba as the primary center of Spanish activities in the Caribbean. In the end, Cuba changed its appearances, as if it was always a Spanish territory. Contrary to popular belief, Havana was not always the capital of Cuba nor its first settlement. Following the struggles with Hatuey, the Spanish established Baracoa as their first capital in Cuba in 1511. Guantánamo Province which contains the municipality of Baracoa was the first Spanish settlement in Cuba. According to some legends, Baracoa was the first place in Cuba where Columbus landed. Regardless of the veracity of this historical event, the isolation and charm of this location made it a haven for illegal trade in the 16th and the 17th centuries.

In 1514, Havana (San Cristóbal de la Habana) was founded. A very small settlement at that time, it would grow into one of the most bon vivant cities in the Caribbean. By the early 1600s, Havana had grown to become the trading post for the Spanish Armada to get gold in exchange for their imports. The Spanish quickly learned the essentials of tobacco production and its consumption in the form of cigars. Also, Havana offered much needed provisions for the Spaniards to extend their explorations into the New World. In 1523, Emperor Charles V authorized 4000 gold pesos for the construction of cotton mills.

By this time, most of the native population had died; many of those who remained were uncooperative. Thus, the Spanish were faced with severe labor shortages. The continuing growth of Havana was driven primarily by the hard toil of the slaves imported from Africa in the latter half of 1500's. Despite all the promises offered by Cuba, according to some accounts the Spaniards considered the island only as a strategic stop en route to the New World. Not until 1553 did the Governor of Cuba relocate to Havana from Baracoa.

The need to protect mainland Cuba from further invasion provoked the Spaniards to construct a fort. Castillo de San Pedro de la Roca near Santiago de Cuba was completed by 1600. Captain Christopher Myngs of the English fleet captured Santiago de Cuba for a short while in 1662, when England faced difficulties from Spain in opening up trade with Jamaica. To fend off escalating pirate attacks and invasion by other European powers, the fort was further expanded to around ten kilometers in 1700. A Dutch fleet led by Piet Heyn robbed the Spanish fleet in Cuban waters in 1628 and provided another motivation for the expansion of the fort. Castillo de San Pedro de la Roca is the only example of this type of Spanish-American military architecture. The fort was restored to its current condition during the 1960s and is now a UNESCO World Heritage Site.

The Cuban resurgence as a key sugar producer in the nineteenth century was a remarkable episode in its history. Prosperity returned to Cuba. Additionally, the massive influx of African slaves changed the demographic and cultural profile of Cuba. Spain's renewed attention in Cuba due to its perceived economic opportunities also meant a further delay in its liberation. Spanish trade laws prevented Cuba from adopting new sugar production and processing technologies. Another impediment to trade development occurred in 1603 when the Spanish government made the sale of tobacco to foreigners an offense punishable by death.

There was an interim period in Cuba's history from 1756 to 1763 when Great Britain showed interest in the island. During this period, Britain warred with France around the world as each nation strove for total dominion. The British navy overpowered the Spaniards and captured Havana in 1762; they also brought in thousands of slaves. Cuba, given its strategic location, was a bargaining piece in British calculations at that time. However, the British were not interested in the agricultural produce of Cuba and harbored no special enmity against the Spaniards. After a series of international negotiations, Cuba was returned to Spain in exchange of Florida.

SPANIARDS SEARCH WOMEN ON AMERICAN STEAMERS

Fig 1.3 The Spaniards strip search American women on steam ships

Other than military wars and trade wars, one especially unique event that occurred in Cuba was the founding of the University of Havana (Universidad de La Habana) in 1728. Originally established as a religious school with appropriate royal and papal authorizations, it was one of the first higher educational institutes to be founded in the Americas.

Until it changed its mandate to a secular liberal arts institution in 1842, it was known as Real y Pontificia Universidad de San Gerónimo de la Habana (Royal and Pontifical University of Saint Jerome of Havana). During Batista's rule, the university became a fertile breeding ground for revolutionary idealism. Batista forcefully closed its doors in 1956 but the university reopened in 1959 after Castro came to power.

While Cuba bore a significant portion of Spain's burden in the aftermath of her global wars, many people in Cuba began to question the Spanish rule. During and after the Haitian Revolution from 1791 to 1804, thousands of French-Haitian refugees fled to Cuba bringing with them an expertise in sugar refining and coffee growing. The increased wealth of the Creole population made them demand a more active role in Cuba's political processes and governance. The wars against Spain during 1868–78 (The Ten Years War), 1879-80 (The Little War) and 1895-98 (The Cuban War of Independence) created fertile grounds for the sprouting of modern Cuban nationalism.

The Ten Years War is historically important because it led to the Pact of Zanjón, formally ending slavery in Cuba. It also gave Cubans greater freedom of speech and some representation in the Spanish parliament. The pact, however, served mainly as a "truce". New rebellions rekindled the very next year and Spain declined to honor the pact. Simmered aggressions continued until the decisive Cuban War of Independence.

The dissonance in U.S.-Spain relations at this time had multiple nuances. The Cuban War of Independence saw the United States supporting Cuba and led to the much larger Spanish-American War. The U.S. had increasingly realized the strategic importance of Cuba, especially in the context of discussions about developing the Panama Canal. In 1848, the U.S. wanted to buy Cuba and offered Spain $100 million; however, the offer was not accepted.

Military intervention was pursued before and after this unusual detour on the part of the U.S. At least some commentators viewed the 'conspiracies' surrounding the USS Maine against this backdrop. The USS Maine (ACR-1) was an American naval ship sent to protect U.S. interests in Cuba. However, it exploded and sank in Havana Harbor in 1898 at the peak of the Cuban War of Independence. The official investigation concluded the sinking was not the result of an enemy attack. Instead, it was the so-called "yellow press" championed by legendary publishers such as Joseph Pulitzer, who twisted it that way and sounded the war cry. Regardless, this naval incident became a hugely sensitive issue in the U.S. and public opinion favored a comprehensive assault against Spain which ultimately led to the Spanish-American War.

The sinking of the USS Maine in the port of Havana increased American ire toward Cuba. The emergence of the U.S. as the winner in the Spanish-American

War sounded the death knell for Spain's presence in Cuba. At the end of this war, the U.S. acquired The Philippines, Puerto Rico, and Cuba. Direct control did not last long, however: after a few years under U.S. control, Cuba emerged into full nationhood in 1902.

In another vein, the U.S. still maintained a modicum of control over the Cuban affairs. This control was made possible by means of the Platt Amendment, passed by the U.S. Congress in 1901. In the guise of continued protection for Cuba, the U.S. retained certain rights to intervene in the internal affairs of Cuba. For U.S. troops to withdraw from Cuba, the Platt Amendment stipulated eight conditions. The eighth condition stated that Cuba should sign the preceding seven conditions in a treaty with the U.S.

For the benefit of the discerning reader, the amendment is reproduced below:

> That the government of Cuba shall never enter any treaty or other compact with any foreign

power or powers which will impair or tend to impair the independence of Cuba, nor in any manner authorize or permit any foreign power or powers to obtain by colonization or for military or naval purposes or otherwise, lodgment in or control over any portion of said island.

That said government shall not assume or contract any public debt, to pay the interest upon which, and to make reasonable sinking fund provision for the ultimate discharge of which, the ordinary revenues of the island, after defraying the current expenses of government shall be inadequate.

That the government of Cuba consents that the United States may exercise the right to intervene for the preservation of Cuban independence, the maintenance of a government adequate for the protection of life, property, and individual liberty, and for discharging the obligations with respect to Cuba imposed by the treaty of Paris on the United States, now to be assumed and undertaken by the government of Cuba.

That all Acts of the United States in Cuba during its military occupancy thereof are ratified and validated, and all lawful rights acquired thereunder shall be maintained and protected.

That the government of Cuba will execute, and as far as necessary extend, the plans already devised or other plans to be mutually agreed upon, for the sanitation of the cities of the island, to the end that a recurrence of epidemic and infectious diseases may be prevented, thereby assuring protection to the people and commerce of Cuba, as well as to the commerce of the southern ports of the United States and the people residing therein.

That the Isle of Pines shall be omitted from the proposed constitutional boundaries of Cuba, the title thereto being left to future adjustment by treaty.

That to enable the United States to maintain the independence of Cuba, and to protect the people thereof, as well as for its own defense, the government of Cuba will sell or lease to the United States lands necessary for coaling or naval stations at certain specified points to be agreed upon with the President of the United States.

That by way of further assurance the government of Cuba will embody the foregoing provisions in a permanent treaty with the United States.

Cuba amended its constitution to include these conditions in 1901 when it became a self-governing colony of the United States. In continuation, Tomás Estrada Palma, a U.S. front man, was made President of Cuba in 1902. In 1903, Cuba pledged to lease some land for a permanent U.S. base in its territory –

Guantánamo Bay. This island would become notorious many years later after a terrorist attack on the World Trade Center's Twin Towers in New York City on September 11, 2001. Finding "loopholes" in the provisions of the Platt Amendment, the U.S. reoccupied Cuba from 1906 to 1909 and declared it a Provisional Government of the United States. In 1934, the Platt Amendment was subjected to Roosevelt's "Good Neighbor" policy. By 1940, all provisions of the Platt Amendment had been removed from the revised Cuban Constitution except the continued lease of the Guantánamo Bay. Even Fidel Castro's diplomatic attempts to eject the occupants based on the provisions of the Vienna Convention on the Law of Treaties, failed.

Through his activism, the revolutionary author and philosopher José Marti became a symbol of Cuba's bid for independence against Spain in the 19th century. He espoused a puritanical view of both the Spanish and U.S. dominance of Cuba and abhorred both. In his earlier activism, he seemed to have neglected the U.S. as a potential expansionist player. That perspective changed when news began to surface indicating the possibility of the U.S. buying Cuba from Spain because it needed new markets for its industrial products (Marti continued to admire the American way of life and the freedom accorded its citizens). In truth, he argued Cuba's interests were only with other countries in Latin America, no common aspiration or goal linked Cubans with European North Americans. According to some commentators, Marti was the first to promulgate the idea of a broad Latin American identity and consciousness.

Later known as the *Apostle of Cuban Independence,* Marti traveled widely and tried to raise the public conscience in favor of the Cuban independence. He played a major role in various Cuban assaults against Spain during that time. He wanted Cuba to become a democratic republic but believed that could be achieved only by means of a revolutionary process. In fact, the ideological basis of the Cuban Revolutionary Party could be traced to his works. The martyrdom of José Martí in a military action during the Battle of Dos Ríos on May 19, 1895 was a key inflection point. José Martí's mausoleum located in Santa Ifigenia Cemetery in Santiago de Cuba is now an important tourist attraction.

One rarely known, but interesting fact, about the U.S.-Cuba relationship in this period is the Havana Special train. This *rail by sea train service* ran from New York to Havana. Even though the segment from Key West to Havana was conducted as a ferry service, the Florida East Coast Railway Company sold tickets all the way to Havana. The train operated for over 20 years, until a hurricane devastated the Miami - Key West stretch in 1935. During its operations, various tour operation companies based in the U.S. offered their "winter escape tours" to Cuba. Some packaged itineraries included Cuba, Jamaica, and Panama.

During this time, Cuba also boasted of its elegant high-end hotels with top of the line luxuries.

Peninsular and Occidental Steamship Company, a British logistics business that began in the early 19th century, offered both cargo and passenger traffic to Cuba. Their steamship SS FLORIDA sailed multiple weekly trips from Miami and Key West. The New York and Cuba Mail Steamship Company (also called The Ward Line) operated shipments from 1841 until 1954. For an interim period, it was also called the Cuba Line. It acquired its competitor, Alexandre Line, in 1888. Later growth was hampered by a series of mishaps and increasing competition from airliners. Standard Fruit & Steamship Company, operating under the name of the Vaccaro Line, offered cruises from New Orleans to Havana. Their all-inclusive weekly tours to Cuba and Panama were advertised for less than $100. The Munson Steamship Line started as a freight line in 1899; but in 1919, it also offered passenger traffic between from New York and

Havana. Until the time of Castro, railroad companies in the U.S. collaborated with steamers to create a seamless cargo and passenger network between the continental U.S. and Cuba.

Cuban aviation has a remarkable history. Cuba was a founding member of the UN conference that created the International Civil Aviation Organization (ICAO). Also, Havana hosted the 1945 conference that led to the creation of International Air Transport Association (IATA). Havana's José Martí International Airport was inaugurated in 1929. Compañía Aérea de Cuba (established in 1919), Compañía Aérea Cubana (est. 1920), and Compañía Nacional Cubana de Aviación Curtiss (estd. 1930), all based in Cuba, were some of the earliest airline companies in Latin America. Airline companies like Servicio Cubano de Aviación, Líneas Aéreas de Cuba, and Compañía Nacional Cubana de Transporte Aéreo also started operations during this time. However, none of these airlines survived more than a few years.

The Curtiss aviation training school began training Cuban pilots in the 1910s. Many world-renowned aviators of that time were fascinated with the Cuban skies. Some flew single engine flights to places as far as Spain. Yet, civil aviation in Cuba until the 1940's largely remained as a means of time sensitive goods traffic, an enabler of business travel to the factory sites located in various provinces, or an elite recreational activity.

Cubana de Aviación survived hard economic times but was acquired by Pan American Airways in 1932. Pan Am had its own scheduled services from the Florida Key West to Cuba since the 1920 and the acquisition of Cubana was of strategic importance. Interestingly, the first Cuban revolution in 1933 did not impact Pan Am investments in Cuba. The company continued its expansion and found in Cuba a hub for its further operations to destinations in South America. By the end of the Second World War, Pan Am had divested its majority stake in Cubana; since that time, the airline has remained as a domestically funded enterprise.

Aeromarine West Indies Airways, based in the U.S., began its operations from Key West to Havana in 1920. The record for the first scheduled U.S. international passenger service is credited to them when they launched their Key West to Havana service on November 1, 1920. Even though Pan Am began its services in 1920, regularly scheduled flights were not offered until 1928. As an aside, Aeromarine also operated flying boats.

Long before Cuba appealed to foreigners, it exported pleasures in the form of sugar and tobacco. In the early 1900's, primarily due to Prohibition and the spread of restrictive moral policing in the U.S., Cuba became a more popular destination than any other location in the Caribbean. Numerous steamships plied the route between Cuba and the United States. A burgeoning array of travel writers began to portray the safely kept wonder that was Cuba. Spanish culture, relaxed life, music, cigars, rum, pretty women, night life, and "whatever"! The exotic intrigue, not far from home for Americans, was a unique selling point for Cuba. In 1920, Cuba created its National Tourism Commission with the objective of creating and marketing a distinct sense of identity for Cuban tourism. Yet, free market forces remained loyal to the allure of the dollar.

However, shifting social and economic compasses from time to time kept the fate of Cuban tourism on a roller coaster.

Chapter 2

The Cuban Crony Capitalist Experiment

Born in 1901, Fulgencio Batista y Zaldivar was the central character of this era (Figure 2.1). This man deeply shaped Cuba's course of history during his reigns (1940-1944 and 1952–1959). Amazingly, the character of Batista during his first stint was irreconcilably different than when he returned to power in 1952. Once a widely admired and popular Cuban leader, he was later perceived as a U.S. backed despot. Actually, he assumed power in the 1933 Revolt of the Sergeants and appointed himself chief of the Cuban armed forces. Elected presidents were his puppets: he ran the government from the backroom. In 1940, he was elected President by popular vote.

Figure 2.1 Fulgencio Batista in Presidential attire, circa 1944.

Batista's rule began with a heavy nationalistic and idealistic tone, promising prosperity for every Cuban. He eliminated the nonindigenous Spanish officers from their top positions in the hierarchy of the Cuban army. He raised the status of Afro-Cubans; he tried to unite the political left and right to forge a new Cuba. He prepared a new Cuban Constitution based on the collectivistic ideals of the 1933 revolt that made him a leader and the same was implemented in 1940. In one of history's ironies, Batista suspended many parts of this Constitution when he returned to power in 1952 following a coup d'état. Even more ironically, Fidel Castro highlighted the need to restore the Constitution as a key driver of his own struggle against Batista.

Batista's key achievement was to give Cuba a new constitution. Cuban intellectuals, including university professors and artists, supported him in this effort. The Constitution, approved in 1940, included provision for women's rights, an eight hour work day, and land reform. The Constitution was inspired by the ideals of the 1933 revolution and was truly transformative. Cuba became a fertile ground for new ideas and experiments. Authors like Ernest Hemingway found in Cuba a paradise reimagined.

U.S. corporations were heavily invested in Cuban agriculture and mining. In fact, American businesses controlled more than two-thirds of Cuba's mines and half of its sugar production. As a result, Cubans owned nothing of value while Americans utilized Cuban labor for paltry sums. Industrialists in the U.S. needed to mend ties with Batista. The U.S. administration was gravely concerned that Batista's moves were leaning toward the socialistic mode of development. Strategic diplomatic moves were made to turn the tide.

While the U.S. was initially surprised at Batista's rise to power, that surprise soon turned to affability. The United States found Batista to be a trustworthy ally who could keep Cuba under control. Cuba aligned with the U.S. during the Second World War. He consulted with the U.S. ambassador on every important policy issue. The Second World War made

Batista a greedy man as he profited from arms trades and made millions of dollars. Apparently, the CIA could monetarily bribe him to do what it wanted. He made money by appointing people to key positions in the bureaucracy. The U.S. Mafia built many big hotels in Cuba during this time. Americans were allowed to open gambling and prostitution centers, too.

Not all political observers are in agreement that the U.S. government was aware of the Mafia's activities in Cuba. The existence of the Mafia was not officially confirmed until the testimony given by Joe Valachi, an Italian American Mafia don, to the U.S. Congress in 1963. The FBI did not officially investigate the possible existence of the Mafia until they became aware of the summit in Apalachin, New York on November 14, 1957. A conspiracy theory making the rounds at that time was that FBI director J. Edgar Hoover was being blackmailed by the Mafia with possible evidence of his sexual deviance. Another theory says Hoover found allies in the Mafia because that organization provided valuable support for the U.S. in its activities against fascism in Italy. The Mafia hated Mussolini in Italy because of the controls he imposed on their activities. In any case, Batista was a favorite child for the U.S. authorities (*See* Figure 2.2).

With all the wealth Batista accumulated before and during the Second World War, he decided to leave politics and settle down in Florida. But, his eyes and ears never really left Cuba. The new president could not contain the criminal syndicates. Cuba again became the safe refuge of American gangsters. However, the halcyon times were only for the elites. Increased income disparity made the poor people feel left out. Unemployment reached nearly twenty percent. Even U.S. business interests became wary about protecting their assets in Cuba.

Then came the 1952 Cuban election and Batista was already returning to Cuba to run for president. In the fray, he soon realized his election chances were bleak. Using all the proxies he had cultivated while at the helm in the army, he led a military coup. The coup was successful primarily because he received implicit support from the United States government. People were so fed up with the previous government that they probably saw a ray of new hope in Batista's second coming. Nor did the communists seem to strenuously object to the coup.

Figure 2.2 Batista ((left) with the U.S. Army Chief Malin Craig (middle) in Washington DC

During this part of his rule, Batista was widely perceived to be a puppet of the United States' imperial interests. By his policies, he sided with the rich plantation owners and land owners. The criminal syndicates based in the U.S. also found a safe haven in Cuba. The syndicates smuggled liquor from Cuba and sold it in the States at highly inflated prices. Cuba manufactured authentic liquor using all homegrown materials and became an international success and the home headquarters of the famous Bacardi rum. Although the Bacardi family left the island nation to open the world's largest premium rum in Puerto Rico, Cuba still makes its version of Bacardi rum. The headquarter building is an important Cuban landmark.

Cuban tourism started in the 1920's during the rule of President Gerardo Machado. Later, Fulgencio Batista's rule offered heydays for tourism and its allied industries. Many celebrities from the U.S. visited Cuba. Casinos mushroomed in the 1920's. In the 1950's, Batista pumped huge sums of government funds into contstructing hotels and resorts, many of which featured casinos. Drug trade and prostitution thrived along with these businesses. Hotels like Havana Libre, Riviera, and Capri were built during this time. Most visitors were Americans and these properties provided employment for many Cubans. An estimated 250,000 tourists visited Cuba annually during the 1950's, but this came to a virtual halt when Castro assumed power.

Fig 2.3 A steamer company advertisement

The lower classes starved and many among poor youths turned to gang activities. Anarchy in Cuban streets became such a threat that even Batista could not control the Mafia. Havana came to be known as the 'cheating capital of the world'. Batista's response was to use mafia against mafia. Batista's family alone controlled 10,000 or more slot machines and law and order in the casinos were indispensable for the regime.

It would be incorrect to say that everyone in Cuba was always poor as many reports would imply. Unlike most Caribbean nations, Cuba had a sizable upper middle class and its members pressed the government to address poverty. Thanks to the power of the government-sponsored Mafia, they could now liberally make use of earnings from their plantations, mines, or the hereditary wealth the Spanish bestowed to them. They shopped imported luxury items and drove imported cars. American culture became an integral part of their daily lives.

Meyer Lansky, a Jewish American mob leader and a respected figure among the mafia gangs, was consulted by the Batista regime to further the process of reforming Cuba's gambling business. Documents reveal that Meyer Lansky was encouraged by U.S. agencies to prevail upon some of the quick-paced gaming practices that would rob gullible unsuspecting tourists. In one extreme version, Batista was a puppet of the gang power on the streets powered by the CIA. However, it is more likely that Baptista received millions of dollars from gangsters and their American bosses.

These considerations aside, Lansky welcomed the opportunity to come out of the shadows and live a respectable life in the limelight. He sought attention and applause. The job entrusted to him afforded him these accouterments and much more. Lansky was given a hefty fee to contain malpractices in gambling facilities. He was involved in training and recruiting casino employees. Interestingly, he started a vocational training school to train future casino employees. Table operators experienced in specialized games were brought from the U.S. on work visas; some assumed the roles of teachers in these schools.

Lansky largely succeeded in what he was entrusted to do. Professionalism and the rule of law were reestablished in the gambling business. Cuban casinos became more attractive to American tourists. Lansky and his cronies were there to support him following the 1952 coup.

In the 1940's, Mafia controlled casinos in the U.S. were facing heat from the federal government, especially the Internal Revenue Service (IRS) and the FBI. Ongoing investigations into organized crime would have put many Mafias behind bars for years. Many secretly entertained the idea of moving their operations to Cuba. Multiple meetings were held in Cuba and the U.S. to devise a plan of action. Lansky exploited this situation and brought the cream of the trade from Las Vegas to Havana. This created a substantial brain drain for the gambling business in Nevada. Havana became the new Vegas.

News reports at that time suggest that the crime syndicate was generally perceived to be a blessing.

These men knew how to run a difficult business for profit. They were considered to be respectable professional consultants who used a blend of bribery and strong arm tactics to prevail against their opponents. Cuban gambling laws were changed in 1955 in consultation with these gangsters-turned professionals. Loaded dice were replaced by well-calculated statistical formulae. Only true racketeers could survive the business and these men made decent money after paying all their expenses and taxes.

Huge western style hotels, casinos, and night clubs were built during this time. Regulations were relaxed for importing materials for their construction. Contractors imported much more material than needed and sold the rest on the black market for premium prices. Batista's government directly pumped in its money to help build these magnificent structures. Of course, the properties would remain under governmental ownership; a license fee and a percentage of profit from operations were remitted to the government; but, there was no cost benefit analysis. Licensees paid ample sums under the table and kept further investigations at bay.

Figure 2.4 A quick summary of tourism in Cuba in the 1950'S (From Constantino Arias' photo entitled "The Ugly American").

As these events were taking place, a young revolutionary was in the making. Batista's rule had become an extremely brutal dictatorship. Fidel Castro, after earning his law degree, was a practicing attorney who filed a lawsuit against Batista's coup. The court rejected the case. Disillusioned, many Cubans took to the streets for an armed rebellion. They needed a leader and Fidel filled the void. At various times, Batista witnessed the rise of Castro and tried to attract him as an ally. He even gave Castro an expensive wedding present worth around $1000.

Castro and his followers viewed the casinos run by the American henchmen as icons of corruption and deeply rooted moral degradation. Casino entrances were somewhat hidden in the hotel lobbies. On New Year's Eve 1958, Castro took power. His followers barged into hotels and casinos to erase from history these fortresses of the privileged few. As the demonstrators were pounding the furniture and overturning the slot machines, no police nor army personnel came to intervene. Even weeks before Castro grabbed formal power of the government, the top brass in law enforcement edgily feared the likelihood of riots and massive defection in their ranks. So, cleansing Batista was an easy task for Castro's followers.

However, it would be incorrect to say that Cubans hated the idea of the gambling business. The Cuban State Lottery system (Renta de la Leteria) had survived since the Spanish times through the reigns of Batista and Castro. In addition, various illegal small scale private lottery businesses (la bolita) piggybacked on the official lottery. Both illegal lotteries and the casinos kept feeding payoffs to key government officials so these businesses could thrive unhampered. The popular anguish toward casinos was primarily due to the government funded extravaganza on them and the exclusion of the local people from its benefits. Free riding had caused a proliferation of brothels and flesh trade, too. At one time, more than 10,000 women were employed by around 300 brothels and these were also targeted by Castro's men as examples of American exploitation.

A question that baffles many experts on Cuba is how Castro could defeat Batista's army. On the battlefields of Santa Clara and Verano, the rebels numbered less than 500; Batista's forces should have overwhelmed the opponents with tanks and military aircrafts – especially with a powerful "sugar daddy" in the neighborhood. Even the powerful Roman Catholic Church extended its support to him. A plausible explanation is the moral superiority of the rebel forces.

Some accounts say the friends and relatives of many soldiers were on the rebel side; they took care of the wounded. Many soldiers were not motivated to fight their kith and kin. Troops overlooked orders from their officers. However, there were also tales of widespread rape and destruction by the guerilla forces. Small scale farm owners were victimized by Castro's men; their properties were destroyed, savings robbed, and their women raped.

It is true that the local guerrilla fighters knew the terrain so much better than Batista's soldiers. Also, Fidel was the embodiment of confidence and had the charisma to attract followers. As a result of these factors, Castro's forces quickly increased in size: from a small yacht containing 82 anarchists to a sizeable army of 40,000 soldiers by war's end.

Some hypothesize that covert Soviet training helped Castro's forces advance faster than their moderate size would imply. This is simply conjecture. More mainstream narratives assert that Castro did not seek Soviet support until U.S. agencies actively sought to annihilate him and take over the reins of power. Soon after the revolution, the United States was on the bucket list of countries Castro had to visit soon. In fact, he was in Washington within six months of taking over power.

Against this backdrop, many attempted to portray the political positioning of Batista. Was he a right-wing fanatic? Yes, during a phase. Was he a socialist? Yes, during another phase. Just as Castro was not a communist until he was forced to align with one of the two major poles of geopolitical power, Batista did not have a lifelong ideological position that guided his action. He was a ruthless gambler who knew what moves to make, when to enter and exit the game.

Some think of Batista's rule as a "golden era". They highlight that most Cubans today cannot afford Cuban cigars, Cuban rum, or even Cuban coffee. Professionals like doctors, engineers, and lawyers make far less now in equivalent dollars than their counterparts made under Batista's rule. When Gerardo Machado was President, conga carnival dances were forbidden in Cuba's streets; when Batista came to power, the dances were permitted albeit with a permit. In general, Batista tolerated freedom of expression. According to some political observers, somewhere at the core of his heart, he entertained the socialist image that gave him power for the first time. That was probably one of the reasons why he pardoned Castro and others after they were captured during their failed coup. Due to food rationing and scarcity of spices, Cuban food culture had soon become passe. Even today, the cuisine served in Cuban restaurants lacks variety. Batista's supporters would lament that Cuba was developing rapidly and then suddenly became "frozen in time". A tourist's view of the antics of the past is seen as the loss of more than half a century for entrepreneurial Cubans.

Chapter 3

The Fiddle Magic of Fidel Castro

The revolution led by Fidel Castro was distinct: for the first time in the history of the Americas, there was a socialistic upheaval in a relatively developed country, even without the support of the established global communist leadership. Also, quite unlike other socialist revolutions, the Cuban revolution did enjoy some sympathy from the middle-class bourgeoisie community. In fact, there was not much resistance to Castro from within Cuba, except from Batista's organized military forces. The support against the revolution from an external power, the United States, also makes the Cuban revolution distinct. This chapter continues a discussion of the rise of Fidel Castro from a would be revolutionary to the new leader of Cuba. This period also marked the beginning of a rapid end to U.S. tourism to the island.

The key underlying condition that led to Castro's ascendancy was the disillusionment of the Cuban people with their current conditions. Batista was a man for the elites, and he was beholden to the powerful Cuban and American interests. As the U.S. increasingly intervened into Cuban lives and as Batista began to align more with U.S. interests in order to protect his turf, the differences between what Cubans wanted and what Americans wanted stood in stark contrast. In turn, this caused the majority of Cuban citizens to feel estranged from their country's developmental process.

So, enter Fidel Castro, the man of the people! Here was a leader who grew up as an everyday Cuban. Even though his father was a powerful Cuban businessman at the time of Fidel's birth, Fidel grew up without the trappings of luxuries. He was born out of the relationship between Ángel Castro y Argiz and Lina Ruz González, Angel's family cook. Subsequently,

Angel and Lina had two additional sons and four daughters. Angel legally married Lena in 1943.

Fidel spent his early life in trying economic conditions as a member of the farm workforce, which included Haitian migrant laborers. He was formally baptized according to Roman Catholic tradition and attended Catholic schools. Yet, even as a child, he began to show elements of rebellion and grew up as an atheist. In college, he did not excel as a scholar but rather devoted much of his time to sports. Even though Fidel would call himself a political illiterate, he was active in student political organizations on campus: specifically, he developed a distaste for U.S. interventions in the Caribbean and began to associate with various leftist-socialist movements prominent at that time in Cuba.

Figure 3.1 The tank (Movimiento 26 de Julio);

Figure 3.1 depicts the tank, in memory of 26th of July Movement; this was the first revolutionary movement led by Fidel Castro, on that date in 1953 on the Moncada Barracks in Santiago de Cuba; later morphed into a political party dedicated to overthrow of Batista government; objectives included the distribution of land, nationalization of public services and other reforms; often portrayed as M-26-7.

Fast forward by five years, December 1958 would prove to be a prophetic month in Cuban history. On New Year's Eve, a newly energized Fidel Castro rolled through the streets of Havana and pulled up in front of the newly completed Havana Hilton hotel. There, he and his rebel comrades proclaimed that they were seizing control of the government and returning it to the people of Cuba. Batista, sensing that the end was near, fled the country earlier that day taking with him the contents of the Cuban treasury. Castro assumed control of the Cuban government without firing a single shot.

Figure 3.2 Castro and his revolutionary team marching to Havana, 1959

Castro's famous words "history will absolve me" during the trials for his attack on the Moncada barracks made a remarkable entry into the Cuban history. Within that moment, Castro began to contribute certain exciting chapters to the contemporary history of Cuba. For history to absolve someone, two practical ways are to redefine the future or erase the past. The latter alternative is what the Castro administration did for the most part soon after it assumed power. Objects representing history were either closed down, repurposed, or renamed. While the political intent was that the nation had no interest serving as a vassal state of the United States, administrative actions supporting that intent meant creating a disconnect with history.

Cuban migration to the US can be dated back to the Ten Years' War (Guerro de los Diez Anos) of independence from Spain (1868–1878). With Castro in power, Cubans tried to flee the country en masse. This exodus in its early phase included only the upper middle class and the ultra-wealthy. It was in a climate of fear of widespread reprisals that refugees fled to the U.S. and sought political asylum. Since 1980, however, the lower economic classes have also begun to leave the country. One massive attempt to flee between April 15– October 31,1980 called the Mariel Boatlift, was the result of reduced economic opportunities in Cuba. Some estimates suggest that one-tenth of native Cubans currently live abroad. Many migrants believed Castro's reign would not last long so they maintained strong ties with Cuba in the hope that they could soon return. To their dismay, the regime in retaliation confiscated the properties of everyone who fled the country. Some of these properties were later converted into tourist accommodations.

By 1960, there were widespread rumors that the regime would take children from their parents to indoctrinate them. News also spread that minor boys would be sent to the Soviet Union to serve in labor camps or be compulsorily drafted to serve in the Cuban army. Apparently, the CIA spread these rumors. The subsequent fear and panic led Cuban parents to send their children to the United States.

Called "Operation Peter Pan", this airlift of over 14,000 Cuban minors between 1960 and 1962 was coordinated by Bryan Walsh, a Catholic priest. James Baker, an American curriculum school administrator in Havana, facilitated the travel logistics. As the President's Personal Representative for Cuban Refugees, Tracy Voorhees lobbied with Eisenhower to ensure that the U.S. government helped with the rehabilitation of the children once they landed in the U.S. Relatives of these children in the U.S. sponsored their visas and paid for their airfare. The planning of this effort was done sub rosa and kept secret from the government. In 1962, to further aid this process, the U.S. State Department eliminated the visa requirement for Cuban minors.

The Mariel Boatlift happened when a wave of Cubans sought asylum in the Peruvian embassy and then left the country via the port of Mariel (west of Havana). Castro surprised everyone by removing security guards from the embassy premises making it easy for anyone to seek asylum. However, he called the asylum seekers "scum" and threatened that leaving Cuba would be a one-way trip. Before security personnel at the embassy were removed, asylum was limited to approximately 10,000 people. After security was removed, nearly 100,000 additional asylum seekers flocked to the venue. Within weeks, 125,000 Cuban exiles had boarded shrimp boats or small recreational crafts and reached U.S. shores. Some refugees were captured during their passage by the U.S. Coast Guard and sent back to Cuba. Some boats capsized and lives were lost. Finally, many Americans' accepting attitude changed when it was discovered that among the refugees were criminals and patients from Cuba's mental hospitals.

In the 1950's, Cuba inaugurated mass tourism to the Caribbean and, in terms of tourist numbers, was greatly in the forefront of competitors like Puerto Rico and the Bahamas. Castro's ascent also marked the end of the flamboyant age of Cuban tourism.

Castro did not hold negative feelings toward tourism per se. In fact, at the American Society of Travel Agents (ASTA) 1959 annual convention in Havana, he announced that he wanted to make Cuba the most important tourist marker in the world tourism map. A range of countercurrents prevented that vision from unfolding including Castro's unwillingness to compromise with casino owners, the American embargo, and Soviet connections. In rapid turnaround, everything American in tourism was gone. Tourism properties were nationalized and key U.S. imprints in tourism business were eliminated. In 1957, there were over 272,000 international visitors to Cuba. By 1960, that number dropped to below 87,000. It wasn't that Castro did not want American tourists. The game changer was Eisenhower's retaliation via a U.S. embargo. This made it necessarily harder for even the most spirited American tourists to visit Cuba. By the end of 1968,

Cuba was the destination of a paltry 3,000 international tourists.

Puerto Rico, the nearby U.S. territory, could attract U.S. tourists without difficulty. Americans could come and go there without visa or other travel restrictions. The only way Cuba could compete was by relaxing travel regulations. The Cuban Tourist Commission publicized widely that Americans could travel to Cuba even without a passport. They could even import their cars duty-free. With Castro, that advantage was gone. As international inbound visits declined, Castro found merit in promoting domestic tourism. While this plan had lofty social objectives in addition to economic developmental concerns, the problem was that most Cubans lacked the resources to spend on vacationing. Cuba was divided along the timeless Afro-Cuban vs White Spanish lines: instead of casinos and nightlife, the former slowly became the primary object of the tourist gaze.

It was also during this time that the Cuban government forged a closer relationship with the Soviet Union. The Soviets began to pump the badly needed foreign exchange to Cuba and Cuba began to align itself more and more to the Soviet bloc. The Soviets were more interested in the sugarcane business than in tourism. This, taken together with Castro's continued crackdown on prostitution and gambling, resulted in Cuba leaving the limelight of international tourism.

The nature of the American embargo against the communist wave hitting Cuba is interesting. This preemptive action did not take shape overnight. Rather, a series of legislative attempts taken over multiple decades shaped its current status. Trading with the Enemy Act of 1917 (TWEA) and the International Emergency Economic Powers Act of 1977 amended section 5(b) of TWEA guided the initial promulgations. The Foreign Assistance Act of 1961 Section 620(a), 22 U.S.C. § 2370(a), was also applied.

This act explicitly prohibited assistance of any kind to the Cuban regime at that time. TWEA of 1917 enabled the President to periodically examine the case for assistance. The Cuban Democracy Act of 1992 (CDA) introduced new provisions that would empower the President to incentivize other countries to support the United States in enforcing the embargo. The law also prevented U.S. corporations and their foreign subsidiaries from doing any business with Cuba, except in such rare instances as the export of essential medical supplies.

Trade Sanctions Reform and Export Enhancement Act of 2000 (TSRA) may be viewed as a retraction from some of the earlier regulations. It prevented the President from unilateral punishment sanctions against a foreign country without appropriate Congressional approval. It also contained licensing provisions for agricultural and food export to Cuba. However, credit assistance or financing for exports was expressly ruled out in the Act. Further, this Act prohibited American businesses or persons relating to Cuba as a leisure tourist or a tourism service provider.

The Cuban Assets Control Regulations (CACR) blocked financial transactions with Cuban personnel or institutions, especially those involving travel, remittances, or property acquisition. Periodically, the U.S. Department of Commerce has issued certain Export Administration Regulations (EAR) in pursuance of the Export Administration Act of 1979. Generally, the regulations would deny exports of any kind unless granted exceptional status from the appropriate authorities.

As noted elsewhere in this chapter, the homes of those who fled Cuba were repurposed as tourist homes. In 1976, Canadian Prime Minister Pierre Trudeau became the first leader from the developed West in the Castro era to visit Cuba. His visit lent some credibility to Cuba as a touristic destination. More than the U.S.S.R., it was Canadian and

European investors who pumped a much needed lifeline of resources into Cuban tourism. As these events occurred, Castro's rhetoric touted tourism as an evil and cautioned that Cubans should not aspire to become tourists or even mingle with them. This was the typical case in Cuba: a surge in tourism means further depletion of the limited supply of resources meant for the consumption of the Cubans.

Before concluding this chapter, a hypothetical question: What if Fidel Castro had not been victorious in the upheaval? Would Cuba have become a U.S. territory like Puerto Rico? There is no easy answer given the complex set of forces surrounding international development. The number of Cubans migrating to the U.S. would probably have been far less. By now, Cuba would have morphed into the preeminent gambling capital of the world – replacing venues such as Macao and possibly even Las Vegas. Tourism in other Caribbean destinations would have declined. Of course, Cuba would not have its current touristic allure in the absence of its revolutionary history and socialistic developments. During Batista's regime, sugarcane cutters worked only four months and spent the rest of the year unemployed and in poverty. The uncertainties associated with dependence upon a single industry (and that a seasonally variant one), would not have significantly improved the lives of average Cubans. In fact, tourism development might have created starker economic disparities: rural areas might have been neglected and rural poverty increased multifold.

Regardless, the revolution was inevitable. The preconditions existed, there was no alternative.

Chapter 4

The Communist Development of Cuba

Following the nationalization of American properties in Cuba, the US government decided that it would no longer tolerate Castro and his government. The U.S. government undertook a plan to topple his regime. Two days before the main attack on April 15, U.S. bombers attacked Cuban airfields. On the night of April 17th, Brigade 2506 (a CIA sponsored group composed primarily of Cuban exiles living in the U.S.) landed at a beach named Playa Giron in the Bay of Pigs. They attempted a failed invasion of Cuba on 17 April 1961. Fidel Castro anticipated an invasion because of the previous air strikes and personally led the defense. However, the attack overwhelmed Castro's local revolutionary forces. But within hours, led by José Ramón Fernández, the Cuban army's elite forces managed to reach the battlefield. The invaders were dealt a devastating defeat. Concerned that other nations would perceive that the U.S. was behind the invasion, Kennedy was reluctant to provide further air support. In just three days, many invaders were killed, the rest were caught and jailed. This massive American failure would reaffirm Castro's position in Cuba and increase its reliance upon the Soviet Union. Castro was widely hailed as the "Savior of Cuba".

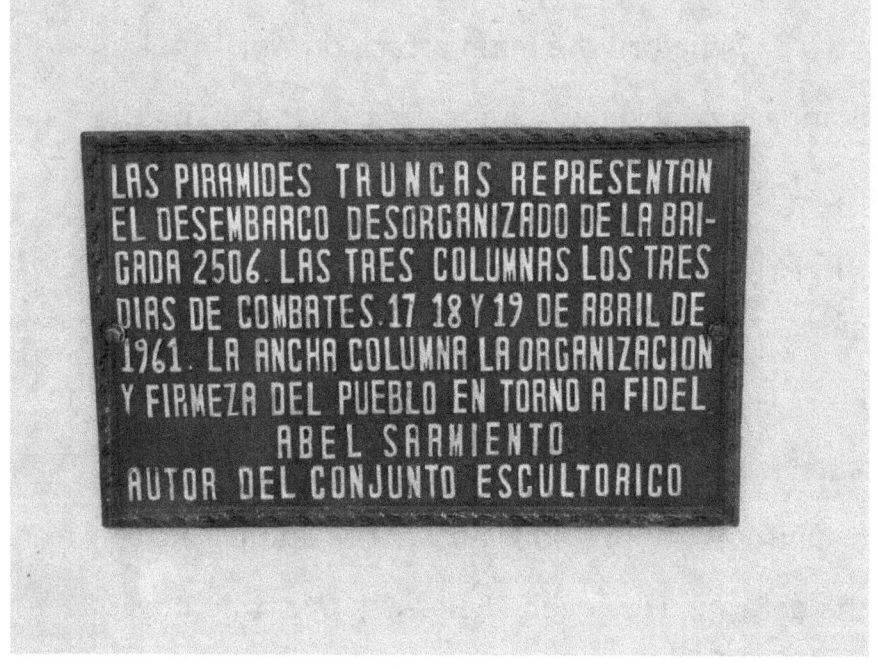

Fig 4.1 The plaque by the Bay of Pigs museum

Before the revolution that brought Fidel Castro to power, tourism's contribution the Cuban economy was second only to agriculture. American investments were pouring in, and Havana was poised to become a *Monte Carlo of the Caribbean*. The Instituto Nacional de la Industria Turistica continued to promote domestic tourism. Again, as in the 1970s, the Cuban government started investing in tour operations and hotel construction in order to attract more tourists from Eastern block countries.

Castro thought agriculture could bolster Cuba's economic well-being even after the decline of tourism. But, Cuba's prominence in sugar production plummeted with the rise in beet based sugar, which was a cheaper and less labor-intensive alternative to cane sugar. Beet sugar was grown in cooler climates and Cuban farmers could not adapt to this environmental challenge. Needless to say, this greatly impacted the country's economy. The decline in the Cuban economy also lead to the migration of people from rural areas to urban centers. As a result, Cuban cities witnessed a boom of Panel Lock ?? houses.

Despite their best planning efforts, the authorities could not find productive employment for all those who migrated to the cities.

These developments highlight an important issue with the Cuban economy: that is, unlike its Latin American counterparts, Cuba has historically lacked a subsistence economy. Both the rural and the urban population were integrated with industrial production. The middle class did try to manage their land, but could do so for only short periods of time. The allure of foreign capital was great. Sugar, tobacco, and coffee farming all followed monopolistic pricing, pegged to the international trade system of the times. Cuba's growth had almost always been debt led, with extensive deficits in the balance of payments. If not for heavily subsidized Soviet aid, Cuba would have struggled mightily to survive the severe liquidity crisis that it faced in 1982.

Castro was steadfast in his ideological commitment to maintain his administration's investments in the social economy. Expenditures in agriculture and industry were more dispensable: Castro believed that the fabric of his socialist society would be endangered if social development commitments were withdrawn. Agriculture and industry could rebound in the next trade cycle, but not a lost faith in the promise of the ideology he held. Two special medium term consequences of this policy were elevated education levels and historically low birthrates of children. These events helped the administration to reduce social sector investments without hampering social development.

Castro's choice of *socialist dependency* rather than *capitalistic dependency* miraculously helped ease the stress on the country's economy without impeding social development. This was the crux of how Cuba was able to get reduce its debt without austerity measures. Comecon / CMEA (1949-1991), the Council for Mutual Economic Assistance, an economic organization under the leadership of the Soviet Union and comprised of countries of the Eastern Bloc along with several socialist states elsewhere in the world, was Cuba's best hope to overcome its burgeoning debt to western nations.

With few alternatives at hand, Castro began to recognize the benefits of a closer nexus with the Soviets. Initially, Castro was reluctant to admit his communist leanings but it became evident when his brother Raul was invited to Moscow to negotiate a sugar export deal. Soon, the Soviet Union replaced the United States as Cuba's number one trading partner. As time passed, Castro's moves became more socialistic. Soviet technologies in agriculture and industry were tailored to keep everyone in the workforce which was exactly what Castro needed. Even today, albeit it with modifications, Cuba remains one of the last stanchions of socialism.

Fig 4.2 The historic Castro-Khrushchev embrace

Just as much as Cubans reclaimed their freedom from the U.S. imperialism, the Soviet socialist influence meant the surrender of Cubans' individual freedom for the collective well-being of the Cuban State. Cubans were taught the importance of sacrificing individual aspirations for the prosperity of the State. Individual property rights were scrapped for the purported well-being of the State. Soon after the American embargo took effect, Cuba learned the importance of self-sufficiency. It would be necessary to rapidly diversify and engage in Import-Substitution Industrialization (ISI). Diversification would reduce the efficiency resulting from specialization. Forging connections with Comecon countries helped Cuba return to specialized production. Comecon's socialist international division of labor meant Cuba could trade its sugar for goods being produced in other Comecon member countries. The Soviet Union also took unprocessed cane sugar from Cuba during off peak seasons so its factories would not be idled.

Despite these measures, Cuba could not amass significant foreign exchange. Trade with Comecon was more in line with a barter system. Thus, the Castro administration had to refocus on the export of services. Maritime transportation and tourism were given special attention and assistance. Cuba also exported specialized labor to various international locations: Cuban government agencies signed contracts for overseas skilled labor development. And, Cuba reportedly sold a portion of what it imported from the Soviet Union at a steep profit. The United Nations Conference on Trade and Development (UNCTAD) in a 1982 report was optimistic about Cuba's growth in services areas such as tourism and healthcare despite the absence of the powerful U.S. market. To the surprise of many, tourists from the U.S. to Cuba reached 200,000 in 1984. As a result, 70 million pesos of hard currency were injected into the economy.

After the Bay of Pigs fiasco, U.S./CIA changed its strategy in dealings with Fidel Castro. It was decided to use the Mafia to kill Fidel. But Mafia gangsters did not kill him; rather, they acted as double agents with the hope of regaining control over their casinos. Marita Lorentz, a German-born American woman and Fidel's former lover, was also persuaded to kill him. Marita was sent to the hotel where Fidel was stationed with poisoning pills. She changed her plans at the eleventh hour and left the hotel room after mending ties with him. However, constant threats on his own life prompted Castro to find an alternative "godfather".

From the earliest days of his involvement in the Cuban revolution, Che Guevara dreamed of making Cuba a model of communism. Although born as an Argentinian, Che was appointed the Minister of Industry in Castro's administration. Castro depended upon Che, considered him a mentor on various issues. He was fascinated by the promises of socialism. Castro feared direct U.S. military intervention and sent Che to Moscow to request help but not for trade negotiations as official statements advertized. Instead, it was to covertly request U.S.S.R. military protection for Cuba. Soviet nuclear missiles were to be installed in strategic locations in Cuba. The U.S.S.R. was initially resigned to the idea that Central and South America were not going to be in their "business plan". In fact, Khrushchev thought Cuba was an untrustworthy CIA representative and diverted Soviet representatives to China.

Fig 4.3 Puente de Bacunayagua in Mantanzas Province

Taking a short detour, it must be reiterated that Cuba did have its fair share of economic development stories. For instance, Figure 4.3 is a photo of Puente de Bacunayagua in Mantanzas Province ; construction began in 1957 and dedicated in 1959 by Fidel Castro; considered the greatest achievement of Cuban civil engineering; It is the longest (1030') and highest (338') bridge in Cuba; it is built across a canyon that separates the sea from the Yumuri Valley (Valle del Yumuri) between Havana and Varadero.

Soviets providing military aid to Cuba was possibly a win-win situation for both parties. It helped the Soviet Union expand its global footprint to the Caribbean basin. It also provided Cubans a sense of security from potential American aggression. Perhaps most importantly, it provided Cuba with a consistent source of hard foreign exchange and much needed employment for its citizens.

The growing Soviet presence in Cuba caused the U.S. grave concern. That concern reached its climax in October 1962 with the discovery of a nuclear capable missile infrastructure in Cuba. U.S. forces blocked an entire shipment of intermediate range nuclear ballistic missiles. After a series of negotiations with the U.S. administration lasting thirteen days, the Soviets finally agreed to turn the shipment back and dismantle the existing missile infrastructure in Cuba.

The agreement meant that the U.S. would not attack Cuba unless directly provoked.

Cubans felt the U.S.S.R. failed to keep its promise when they withdrew the missiles. Castro heavily criticized the U.S.S.R. for its actions. Later, he was invited to Moscow in state honor. If Che's visit to the U.S.S.R. led to it supplying nuclear missiles, Castro's visit there after the Cuban missile crisis helped thaw the deteriorated relations when the U.S.S.R. withdrew its missiles. In later years, Che suspected the U.S.S.R. was slowly moving toward capitalism. He criticized the Soviet model for its close-ended posture and its averseness to free thinking. He favored central planning and disavowed how the Soviet Union blended business autonomy and profit seeking with central planning. He felt it denigrated human beings to be motivated to work for the selfish urge for profit. Che wanted the State to provide its people with decent living conditions and meet their basic needs in return for their contribution to the well-being of the

State. Che's pressure upon Castro to stay away from the U.S.S.R., and Castro's compulsion to retain the alliance with the U.S.S.R., meant that Che would have to relocate elsewhere to further shape his revolutionary ideas.

Fig 4.4 The Soviet/Russian embassy in Havana (Source: Nick De Marco, www.nickdemarcofoto.com)

The bonhomie with the Soviet bloc helped resurrect Cuban tourism in the 1970s. Increasing numbers of visitors from the Soviet bloc began to flock to Cuba. The Havana Hilton (later renamed as the Habana

Libre) and the Riviera were the last two American hotels. These two icons and the other existing hotels were not sufficient to accommodate the needs of the new visitors and a building boom ensued.

The Soviet Union invested heavily in building the much needed hospitality infrastructure. Newly constructed hotels were modest in appearance, mindful of the austere expectations of typical visitors. Six hotels were completed in 1976, nine in 1977, and eight in 1978. In 1979, the total number of tourists visiting Cuba reached nearly 130,000 and over 300,000 by 1989.

Cuba has long depended on imported fuel. Nuclear energy was entertained as a possibility as early as 1956 when the island nation signed a cooperative agreement with the U.S. to develop it for civil uses. However, less than three years later Fulgencio Batista's regime was overthrown by Fidel Castro. U.S.-Cuba relations were severed and the agreement never implemented. However, the Soviet Union entered an agreement with Cuba to construct twelve reactors at three sites: Cienfuegos (south central), Puerto Esperanza (west), and Holguin (east) . In the end, it was decided to build only two 440 megawatt nuclear reactors in Juragua near Cienfuegos and the site's worker suburb of"Ciudad Nuclear" was established. Construction began on the first reactor in 1983, the second two years later. The first reactor was projected to be completed in 1995 or early 1996. When the Soviet Union collapsed, its financial assistance to Cuba ended and the projected halted.

Several attempts to reach a financial agreement to complete the project failed because Fidel announced Cuba would be unable to meet the financial obligations. If completed, the project was frought with problems, a possible Chernobyl in the making: inferior construction, lack of training for Cuban engineers to operate and provide maintenance on the Soviet reactors, no coherent method of nuclear material disposal (in fact, the plan was simply to discharge waste into the surrounding waters), and discharge of radioactive materials into the air would threaten the Caribbean as well as southern Florida. Today, the nuclear facility is a rusting ruin visible across the bay from Cienfuegos, a reminder of the abject failure of an attempt to supply a significant amount of the annual fuel requirement of Castro's Cuba. Cuba's once dependable trading partner, Venezuela, is no longer able to supply much needed oil in exchange for Cuba's medical assistance due to political unrest and failed government policies.

Political tourism was a major form of tourism during this period. In its purest form, this type of tourism occurs when sympathizers of international political struggles travel to destinations of struggle to express solidarity with that struggle. However, tourism to Cuba from the Eastern bloc was primarily to achieve a better understanding of its unique socialistic development. The source and destination governments incentivized this touristic venue as tourists did not want their money to go into capitalist pockets. Visitors to Cuba were presented with a fascinating view of how the state controlled tourism resources, products, infrastructure, and management in a comprehensive manner.

Guest-host interactions were limited and the official line stressed that the interactions would adulterate culture and values. Of course, the real reason was to prevent the free flow of ideas which the government feared would inflame dissent. Cuban residents constantly felt the pain of exhibiting a life of freedom and abundance to tourists. In an otherwise collectivistic society, everyone began to distrust each other and considered them to be secret government agents. Yet, given the similarities in the institutional characteristics of socialist countries, tourists from the Eastern bloc felt at home when they traveled to Cuba. Most socialist countries had adopted, in some form or other, the administrative systems originally developed by the Soviet Union.

Given the political need for the controlled flow of ideas, Cuba encouraged group tours. Tourist groups were escorted to particular locations with the implicit objective of showcasing specific achievements of the state. Thus, tourists were led to museums, housing projects, factories, farms, universities, and defense facilities where the narrative was facilitated with the help of government employed interpreters. The vibrancy of social institutions and how that could not have been achieved without a revolution was always at the center of the narration.

In the 1960s and 1970's, some of the dissenting minority voices in the United States also found a champion in Cuba and the most curious took trips to Havana. During their tours, they were shown how America's policies victimized Cuba and how resilient Cubans stood against the U.S. led tyranny. Even some progressive church groups sent their leaders to Cuba where they were impressed with the humility of the people. Tourists did not see, or chose not to see, the subjugation of individual liberties, the persecution of sexual minorities, poverty, despotism, etc., in Cuba. Finally, those Americans who were not supportive of their own government's policies actively sought alternatives; they glorified the alternative found in their next door neighbor ninety miles from the United States. Many western intellectuals felt alienated in their own lands and found appeal in the developments of the Cuban political economy. These political pilgrims from the U.S. became a key source for Cuba in garnering vital foreign exchange, too.

By 1985, the Soviet Union was reassessing its overseas commitments. Cuba was receiving nearly $4.5 billion a year from U.S.S.R. in the form of developmental and military assistance. This financial arrangement was untenable for the crumbling Soviet economy. Castro was diverting part of the aid to support proletarian revolutions and regimes in other parts of the world. Ironically, this was not viewed favorably in the U.S.S.R. Castro's imprints on international proletarian movements at the expense of U.S.S.R. invited their discord. In 1988, Castro was forced to withdraw his forces from Angola. Cuba seemed to have anticipated the weakening of the Soviet Union. As early as 1988, talks were held in Havana to discuss ways of mending relationships with the U.S. What happened however was a thaw in U.S.-USSR relations. Why? Because when Mikhail Gorbachev came to power as the President of the Soviet Union, he made friendly overtures to the U.S. However, this did not help with U.S.-Cuba relations. The widespread political sentiment in the island nation was that nothing less than the absolute demise of the Castro regime would be acceptable.

Chapter 5

Decades of Uncertainty

Cuba is one of the few countries in the world that has transitioned, although imperfectly, through all the four phases of socioeconomic development that Karl Marx hypothesized. The demise of the Soviet Union in 1989, and the subsequent dissolution of Comecon, brought rapid and dramatic change to the people of Cuba. It inaugurated the "Special Period" (*Período Especial*). Imports and exports dropped by about 80%; GDP declined by 30%. This also marked the beginning of the new era of Cuban international tourism. The disintegration of the Soviet Union forced Castro to find other means of economic survival. He allowed Cubans in the U.S. to send money back home to support families. He also allowed small businesses to be established in certain sectors (most remain under Army control).

Fig 5.1 A typical rural street view

The collapse of the Soviet Union was accompanied by
the departure of Soviet investments in Cuba. The
"Special Period" was characterized by near economic
collapse in Cuba. The Cuban government, which had
been the sole provider of the fundamental needs of its
citizenry, came under intense economic and social
pressures. Food shortages and outages were
common, gas prices peaked, citizens literally lined up

to secure their rationed pound of rice, public services were curtailed or eliminated, and hospital services deteriorated. Castro withdrew the remaining foreign currency savings in order to import bicycles from China. These bicycles were freely distributed to people for their shared use.

Reliance upon tourism for economic survival is a popular alternative chosen by newly liberated and ex-socialist countries. The transition to a market oriented economy in those countries is often inaugurated with unbridled tourism promotion as tourist dollars provide a quick jumpstart to the economy. Tourism also infuses professional values such as customer service into the workforce. Finally, tourism development can stimulate infrastructure development in areas such as transportation and communication.

The Castro administration's final economic restoration measure in the 1990's was a refocus on tourism. Oil imported from Venezuela was calculated to stimulate the Cuban economy: however, heavy reliance on Venezuelan resources had its limits. Tourism businesses were reopened in massive numbers. Even U.S. citizens could visit Cuba albeit by first flying to another country. The majority of clientele came from Europe, South America, and Canada. By 1993, tourism numbers had risen to a whopping 600,000. Two years later, Cuba's annual tourism revenues surpassed 1billion USD and by the end of the following year, the number of visitors grew to over 1 million. Canadians constituted the largest visitor base, over one-quarter of a million.

The expectations of the new tourists to Cuba were different from those of the Soviet or Eastern bloc visitors. New kinds of hotel rooms, new attractions, and new tourist support facilities were needed. Numerous all-inclusive properties were developed to cater to the new tourist segments. Since the Cuban government did not have the requisite money to invest, joint ventures with international investors was allowed. Spain emerged as the prime trading partner in tourism. Even though foreign investors supplied all the funding, the joint venture was framed as if it was a Cuban majority venture. The Cuban government's 51 percent or more of the stake in these ventures ensured continued State control over the industry.

The boom in tourism resulted in a severe shortage of service personnel (bartenders, waiters, house keepers, etc). Wages and tips were attractive in the tourism industry. Tips paid in the foreign currency enabled hospitality workers to afford the luxuries unavailable to other Cubans. A school teacher earning 200 Cuban pesos a month could earn the same amount in a day as a waiter. Those employed in professional capacities (doctors, engineers, lawyers, etc.), abandoned their State supported jobs and turned to these newfound opportunities.

The "brain drain" from key scientific professions was so alarming that the government had to formalize employment requirements to work in the tourism industry. This led to the development of hospitality education certification and licensing. Hospitality job aspirants had to apply and be accepted into one of the training schools. The length and intensity of the training programs and the admission requirements disincentivised people in other professions to join the hospitality trade.

School authorities directed the candidates to various specialized areas in the industry. The schools also assigned their graduates to work at particular properties. The Cuban government collected a management fee in foreign currency from the overseas hotel investors but the wages of the Cuban workers were paid by the government in Cuban pesos. Elements of centralized vocational planning percolated throughout this process.

The "Special Period's" austerity requirements became unbearable and forced Cubans to look for opportunities outside the formalized economic peripheries. Prostitution became a prime economic avenue. During Batista's rule, prostitution was prevalent among poor rural women. Just before Castro came to power, there were more than 100,000 prostitutes in Cuba and thousands of men found employment as pimps. This arrangement prevailed until Castro came to power when it suddenly stopped. With tourism re-instated as the epicenter of economic development in the 1990's and beyond, its undesirable facets resurfaced. Tourism exacerbated wealth differences, equivalent master-slave social relationships, and prostitution reappeared as a primary manifestation of the same. Tourists could take prostitutes to *casas particulares* rentable for less than ten dollars (most established hotels still don't allow the service of prostitutes). It is not uncommon for Cuban police officers tracking prostitutes to collect bribes to augment their skimpy salaries instead of enforcing the laws. The proliferation of "love hotels" benefitted the locals, many of whom lived in squalor. With children often in the household, making love was constrained. After putting aside some savings, Cuban couples could rent rooms in government / military owned motels called *posadas* for hourly rates to engage in intimate relationships. Sometimes clients could conduct their liaisons in private rooms for a little over five dollars for three hours.

The term *jineterismo* refers to illegal economic activities related to tourism in Cuba. While prostitution and pimping were not legalized, they continued to thrive without police interference. Jineterismo appeared in various other forms such as unregulated tour guiding, informal renting of personal cars, and selling counterfeit goods. Jineteros, those who practiced jineterismo, spoke English and became the interface between tourists and the Cuban people. Even during the embargo, Spaniards and Canadians sought prostitutes; some explicitly demanded underage boys and girls. In the "Special

Period", sex tourism and child sex tourism skyrocketed. Cuba was cheaper. It was close, especially for those in the North America. Cuba's achievements in public health meant prostitutes were less likely to have STDs.

Cuban agriculture did not experience a significant recovery in the "Special Period", despite the government's untiring efforts. During the period of Soviet reliance, Cuban export opportunities in sugar led to the abandonment of other crops. The monoculture in sugar production stifled agricultural diversity. Urban migration during that period also resulted in a scarcity in the agrarian workforce in rural areas. Castro banned deep sea fishing for fear of citizens fleeing the country and the fish supply in Cuba was limited to fishing farms. Cows were strictly designated as commercial meat; to kill and eat a cow was a severely punishable offense. Even when agricultural production resumed, Cuba lacked the technologies to make that production efficient.

Figure 5.2 A depiction of the countryside

The absolute lack of private property rights intimidated even those farmers who could invest their personal means into agricultural technologies. Government controlled communist business units called UEBs sold products at prices the government dictated: UEBs had to purchase products from farmers at rock bottom prices in order to meet the governmental expectation of selling the produce to consumers at very low prices. Farmers suffered huge losses in this financial arrangement and it served as a major disincentive for private investment in farming.

Climatic conditions in Cuba were also a factor. Some progress was made in agrarian production: mangoes, banana, guava, cucumber, avocado, etc. According to some reports, nearly thirty percent of the crops produced in rural areas rotted and never reached urban areas – poor distribution and substandard warehousing facilities were blamed. Rice, the most important of all food crops, continues to be imported in substantial quantites.

Some of these analyses could be challenged depending on one's perspective. The World Wild Fund, in its 2006 report, praised Cuba for achieving its sustainable development goals. Rejecting the use of chemicals and machinery led to ecologically friendly forms of agriculture in which nature and culture coexisted. Developments in agriculture in Cuba in the "Special Period" were economically unsound but ecologically sustainable.

Cuba is noted for its "one country – two currencies" policy. The Cuban peso (CUP), the currency in which

Cuban citizens are paid, was complemented with another currency in 1993: the Cuban convertible peso (CUC). The CUC is pegged at 1:1 to the USD and is approximately 25 times more valuable than the CUP. So, foreign tourists convert USD to CUC to spend while in Cuba. Many items are priced higher in CUC; on the other hand, most Cubans continue to buy lower priced local items in CUP. Since CUC is a closely controlled currency, it holds no value outside Cuba. Yet, this monetary anomaly reduces price inflation that accompanies international tourism development in other underdeveloped countries. In November 2004, the U.S. dollar was no longer accepted in Cuban retail outlets; this left the convertible peso (CUC) as the only currency in circulation in Cuban businesses. The CUC is a dichotomized symbolization of the rise of Cuban tourism and its agrarian decline. Young Cubans have found a way to earn in CUC, convert to CUP, and then use that currency to buy food and other amenities that the government distributes at heavily subsidized rates.

It is not uncommon for business owners to collect USD or EUR for services and then use black market channels to send them to safe havens abroad. It is becoming increasingly apparent that Cuba will revise its monetary system which might mean a total / phased abolition of the CUC currency. The International Monetary Fund (IMF) has also warned Cuba to get rid of CUC if it wants to marketize its economy.

(A practical tip: there is a conversion penalty of 10-13% while converting USD to CUC; so, tourists are advised to bring EUR or CAD).

International tourism and visitors to Cuba expanded dramatically, pouring much needed hard currency into the island's coffers. However, as noted elsewhere, the hemisphere's largest and most wealthy visitor base, the United States., was very minimal in presence. The big growth in international tourism to Cuba was accomplished without U.S. customers and industry players. The first new property opened in Cuba in the post-Soviet era was the Spanish-based Melia properties owned Cohiva hotel. The all-inclusive properties boom has continued in Havana, Varadero, and neighboring areas, but with no U.S. or U.S.S.R. presence. This is a remarkable period, in that respect. Cuba now faces the need to attract revenue from tourists originating in countries other than their original sources. Austere properties have given way to beach holiday centered 'sun and fun' properties. Spain continues to maintain its key investor status, but countries like Mexico, Canada, Jamaica, UK, and Germany have shown interest in Cuban tourism.

All-inclusive resort based tourism meant less spending outside these properties and less movement of tourists. By international comparison, these properties were priced low and hence became very popular for price conscious tourists. Despite significant quality improvements, there existed little product differentiation across these properties. Market segmentation did not exist, for the most part. This period also saw the beginning of resort development in the Cuban cayos, such as Cayo Coco, Cayo Guillermo, and Cayo Laro. These venues added an extra flair to Cuban tourism.

International Terminal 3 of the Jose Marti International Airport in Havana was built in 1998. This addition tremendously expanded international connectivity to Cuba. In similar fashion, secondary airports such as those in Varadero and Santiago de Cuba began to cater to international airlines. It now became much easier for an international traveler to reach Cuba.

Notwithstanding Cuba's distaste for capitalism, there has been experimentation with variants in the private sector. These primarily include self-employed single entrepreneurs, private farmers, agricultural co-operatives, and non-agricultural cooperatives. Self-employment is available in 201 strictly defined categories. Joint ventures in Cuba are neither in the private sector nor in the government sector. Since more than half the ownership stake in them is with the government, it is more accurate to classify them as state-owned. Employees in these joint venture companies are sourced from a government controlled employment exchange, too.

Politically, the demise of the U.S.S.R. should have compelled the United States to show renewed interest in Cuba. But, that did not happen. The U.S. apparently neglected developments in Cuba even after the Soviets withdrew. This poses the question: Was there anything intrinsically great in Cuba or did fear of the Soviet bloc's eschew that possibility?

Chapter 6

The Second Coming of the United States

U.S. - Cuba relations changed dramatically in December 2014, when U.S. President Barack Obama announced the restoration of diplomacy with Cuba and the reopening of the U.S. embassy in Havana. President Obama also publicly vowed to sweep aside the last remnants of the "Cold War". With this announcement came an easing of restrictions on banking, remittances, and travel for Americans. The will of Cuban people for more economic freedom and the need of the Cuban State to seek the support of capitalistic enterprises for development interacted to make this finally happen. Obama's personal philosophy of a more integrated world with porous national boundaries also helped this new accord.

Fig 6.1 Raul Castro with Barack Obama when the latter visited Cuba in March 2016.

Cuba has a significantly successful history of clandestinely promoting self-employment in the private sector, especially during periods of recession. Recent changes should provide added impetus to private business endeavors, but Cuba has considered a move toward capitalism. The best official explanation for all the recent changes in Cuba is that the country is transitioning toward a more participative form of socialism, reform socialism, or decentralized socialism: socialism of the people, for the people, by the people.

Although not directly related to the embargo, special credit should be accorded to the Obama administration's for the short-lived "Wet Foot/Dry Foot" Policy for Cubans. Per this policy: If Cuban migrants traveling to the U.S. are intercepted at sea, they are sent back to Cuba or a third country; if they are able to land on U.S. soil before being apprehended, they are offered a pathway to U.S. residence and eventual citizenship. This policy, however, was rescinded in January 2017.

When President Obama extended the "olive branch" to Cuba, stocks and index funds with exposure to Cuba like $CUBA soared. Many remembered the "wet days" of capitalism during Batista's time when per capita income reached levels comparable to some of the developed countries and economic growth proceeded seemingly on nonstop upswings. On September 27, 2016, President Obama announced his pick for Ambassador to Cuba, the first such U.S.

diplomatic appointment in over fifty years. The move

was received with pervasive optimism.

WASHINGTON
June 30, 2015

His Excellency
Raul Castro Ruz
President of the Council of State
  and the Council of Ministers
  of the Republic of Cuba
Havana

Dear Mr. President:

I am pleased to confirm, following high-level discussions between our two governments, and in accordance with international law and practice, that the United States of America and the Republic of Cuba have decided to re-establish diplomatic relations and permanent diplomatic missions in our respective countries on July 20, 2015. This is an important step forward in the process of normalizing relations between our two countries and peoples that we initiated last December.

In making this decision, the United States is encouraged by the reciprocal intention to develop respectful and cooperative relations between our two peoples and governments consistent with the Purposes and Principles enshrined in the Charter of the United Nations, including those related to sovereign equality of States, settlement of international disputes by peaceful means, respect for the territorial integrity and political independence of States, respect for equal rights and self-determination of peoples, non-interference in the internal affairs of States, and promotion and encouragement of respect for human rights and fundamental freedoms for all.

The United States and Cuba are each parties to the Vienna Convention on Diplomatic Relations, signed at Vienna on April 18, 1961, and the Vienna Convention on Consular Relations, signed at Vienna on April 24, 1963. I am pleased to confirm the understanding of the United States that these agreements will apply to diplomatic and consular relations between our two countries.

Sincerely,

Fig 6.2 Obama's letter to Raul Castro, announcing a new beginning

Despite this, the embargo remains in place – only its implementation has been relaxed. Americans traveling to Cuba must still fall into one of the approved visa categories. The twelve categories of authorized travel to Cuba are: family visits; official business of the U.S. government, foreign governments, and certain intergovernmental organizations; journalistic activity; professional research and professional meetings; educational activities; religious activities; public performances, clinics, workshops, athletic and other competitions, and exhibitions; support for the Cuban people; humanitarian projects; activities of private foundations or research or educational institutes; exportation, importation, or transmission of information or informational materials; and certain authorized export transactions. It should be noted that these categories do not include leisure travel. As a result, it is still not legal for U.S. citizens to visit Cuba for tourism purposes. This, coupled with the fact that marketing communication about the policy changes did not reach mass tourists, meant the promise of tourism from the American outbound market did not materialize as much as hyped.

It always has been possible to travel between the United States and Cuba, even during the heights of the embargo. However, this travel was only possible via charter flights, and all passengers had to provide documentary evidence that their purpose of travel fell within one of the twelve approved categories. Additionally, all travel had to be booked through a U.S. licensed travel agent approved to book travel to Cuba. Following the relaxation of restrictions by President Obama, several U.S. flag carriers applied to the USDOT for approval to fly to Cuba. The first regularly scheduled airline to Cuba was JetBlue. Actual demand fell significantly below the increased seat capacity, and the airlines operated with basically empty flights.

 November 2016. The United States has a new president. During the campaign leading to his election as the President, Donald Trump vowed to revise Obama's executive orders on Cuba. Progress made in mending relationships during the previous regime now face reversal as President Trump has announced some policy changes regarding Cuba. Assuredly, more changes will be forthcoming, but are unpredictable. Some critics aver that Trump does not have any animus toward Cuba. In fact, some reports emerged during his presidential campaign suggesting that his companies secretly conducted business in Cuba during the embargo. Many observers believe President Trump will follow his instincts as a shrewd businessman and his decisions will be guided by realpolitik.

Some sources believe that, even after Trump's toughened stance, American businesses will continue to invest in Cuba. A permit from the Office of Foreign Affaird Control (OFAC), an arm of the Treasury Department, is all that is required. As always, the Cuban partner is the government. Hotel property management companies have found this deeply troubling. In typical agreements, the hotel management companies manage the profits and costs associated with the operations as well as employee relations. From a Cuban perspective, the government wants to manage the finances and the employees but pays a fee to a hotel management company for their marketing efforts.

International hotel companies, after their initial enthusiasm, learned this bitter lesson: the untrained Cuban government employees administering the affairs of the hotel, the substandard materials used in the hotel construction, the menial pay the hotel staff receives, or the quality of food and beverages being served in the hotel, over none of which the management company has any control, could still bring them global brand disrepute. If traditional businesses fail, there is a beacon of hope in the emerging sharing economy. Airbnb has been a resounding success, and many foreign tourists seeking authentic Cuban experiences prefer to book accommodations using their services. There is some chemistry of attraction between Cuban socialism and capitalistic sharing.

Multinational businesses such as Unilever, Tyson Foods, Nestle, Anheuser-Busch, Netflix, Samsung, Alcatel, Colgate, Cargill, Accord Hotels, Kempinski, Mitsubishi, Benz, Google, etc. have developed varying degrees of presence in Cuba. A few banks in Cuba now accept payments processed through Mastercard. Coca-Cola is sold in Cuba, although it is imported through its foreign subsidiaries. Russia and China have taken a more strategic approach with regard to investment: Chinese companies have invested heavily in infrastructure projects while Russian companies have partnered with Cuba in some of their advanced pharmaceutical research projects. Empresa de Telecomunicaciones de Cuba S.A. (ETECSA), the government-owned telecom provider in Cuba, has received significant investment from the Chinese telecom giant Huawei.

Cuba joined the World Trade Organization (WTO) in 1995 and announced its intention to conduct business on the global playing field. Would Cuba crumble without international aid? No. Cuba has lower child mortality and higher literacy rates than the U.S. Data available from the World Bank over the last half decade of the development history of Cuba attests to that. Trends in the life expectancy of Cubans, Cuba's GDP growth, and its per capita growth in wealth all remain as positive as they were prior to President Obama's friendly gesture. Racial tensions in Cuba have subsided. To its credit, nearly half the members of the Cuban parliament are women; the same is true of university professors. Significantly, Cuba has nearly eradicated homelessness.

A key area of needed reform is freedom of expression. Cuba downplays this freedom as a capitalist ploy. Cuba is concerned that the Western propaganda will deluge Cuban citizens if uncontrolled access is given to the Western media. Notwithstanding this, in 1996, Sprint-Nextel, based in the United States, inaugurated the first-ever access to the internet for Cubans. The purchase of personal computers was made legal in 2008. With more recent Chinese investments, Cuba is poised to step up its role in the cyber field.

While it can continue its neo-socialist experiment, it is still important for Cuba to mend its relations with the U.S., and not solely for monetary reasons. Historically, the U.S. has exercised its global diplomatic influence to discourage other countries from investing in Cuba. Cuban exiles in Florida, the epicenter of anti-Cuban propaganda in the U.S., continue to lobby against restoring friendly relationships. To that end, during the embargo even some of the most willing European or Canadian businesses could not meaningfully engage with Cuba. Cuba recognizes this.

Raul Castro stepped down from the presidency in April 2018 but will remain in an important administrative position. His successor is Miguel Diaz-Canel, a former university professor and long-time member of Cuba's communist party. It remains to be seen how much freedom he will given to govern since many of the most powerful positions in government will still be occupied by octogenarian military figures from the Revolution.

It will also be interesting to see if Diaz-Canel and Donald Trump can meet on common ground and restore amicable relations. Both countries have much to gain if such a relationship can be forged. Only time will tell. In his first eighteen months in office, President Trump has shown an enthusiasm to meet with heads of state around the world (China, North Korea, Russia, etc.). Meeting with Cuba's President Diaz-Canel could eventually take place if mutually agreed arrangements were developed. The most pressing point confronting the two nations is an embargo which has been in place for nearly sixty years. This embargo has effectively stifled commercial ventures as well as people to people relationships. Underlying the embargo is the basic dichotomy between capitalism and communism. If a meaningful compromise could be forged, it would open the doors to all types of joint ventures and normalize U.S.-Cuba relations under the present administrations.

Fig 6.3 Embassy of the United States in Cuba

What might complicate these developments is that both Russia and China are in expansionist modes. Their presence in Cuba means that Cuba might be able to overcome its economic challenges without overly depending upon the U.S. What if China announces tomorrow that it is going to invest in modernizing the island nation's highway system? With better roads, the movement of agricultural products from fields to urban centers would be faster as would connections to tourist destinations .

Similarily, what if Russia comes forward tomorrow to assist in the renovation and expansion of the aging and neglected infrastructure in the Cuban tourism sector? It is no secret that both Russia and China covet having a military presence in Cuba. It is critically important for the U.S. to make a proactive move by ameliorating the embargo conditions.

Chapter 7

Musings on Cuba – Some Concluding Thoughts

For many tourists, Cuba is a curiosity to be explored; a gem that has remained largely immune to spatio-temporal developments over the past half century. Those interested in the Caribbean, but bored with the the standard recipe of the 4s (sun, sea, sand, sex) tourism, are a unique interest group in Cuba. The first impression of many tourists visiting Cuba is the degree of control over all facets of the economic and social spheres. Succinctly stated, to what do the Cuban people actually have access?

Old Havana (La Habana Vieja) is the number one destination for most tourists. It's in the heart of the original development of Havana and its architecture is dazzling to the eye. Evidence of this is Cathedral de San Cristobal, a landmark dating back to 1748 and designed in the American baroque style. The Plaza de

Armas is a popular meeting point where tourists can shop among the many vendors and craftsmen. The Museum of the Revolution (Museo de la Revolucion) tells in detail the story of the Cuban revolution in thousands of pictures and their accompanying texts. These are some of the most popular sites in Old Havana.

Fig 7.1 Dupont House / Xanadu Mansion, Varadero beach; name derived from the magnificent palace of the great Mongol warrior, Kublai Khan; billionaire Irene Dupont's mansion was built in the 1920s and its

nine hole golf course was the only one of its kind in Cuba until recently).

Hemingway's home in Cuba (Finca La Vigia, or "lookout house") is conveniently located in a nearby suburb of the capital city. It attracts many literary minded tourists (his faithful typewriter is on display in his writing room; his yacht/fishing boat, Pilar, is also found on the grounds).

Vagon Mambi (The Elegant Train of Presidents), located in Old Havana close to the edge of the Harbor, is an interesting train that has not moved in ages but still has an incredible story and history to tell. From the passengers it held to the story behind its name, the history will continue to be told while it is on exhibit at Havanas Historian Office. Mambi dates back to the early years of the 20th century and was best known for being the presidential train of Cuba. Reflecting the golden era of train travel, Mambi was a palace on wheels. Elegant dinning room, a meeting room, and four dormitories equipped with a bathroom, kitchen, freezer and a porch, it truly was unlike anything anyone had seen before. Even the furniture, glassware, table linen, and silverware seen on the train were exquisite and all complemented the look and feel of the train perfectly. Coche Mambi or also referred to as Vagon Mambi was originally built in 1912 in the U.S. with Canadian components. It is one of the few luxury trains ever built. The name comes from the soliders who fought in the Independence War of 1868. The Mambi was retired in 1959 and became a historial artificate for Cuba. The history that happened inside the train, and the way it is presevered, allows people to embrace the past with the present. Visiting the Mambi and seeing its elegance and learning its history is a must while in Cuba.

Another incredible sight in Cuba is the classic cars you see driving around. Cuba is like a rolling car museum. From old Oldsmobiles, Chevys, Buicks and Fords everywhere you look is like a car show featuring all these classic beauties. But why do they focus so much on maintaing these older cars and using them on a daily basises verse buying newer cars? The stuck – in- time feeling has been created after a four decade long grudge held by their late leader, Fidel Castro against the United States. Even though the island of Cuba only is a meager 90 miles from Key West, Florida, Fidel Castro had placed a ban on foreign vehicle imports which made it nearly impossible to buy new parts and fuel for the old-school American cars. It is estimated that there are nearly 60,000 classic American cars that cruise the streets of Cuba. Half of those cars come from the 1950s, 25 percent are from the 1940s, and the remaining 25 percent come from the 1930s. As a visitor, you can ride around in these classic cars or have one as your rental while you are staying in Havana.

The mainstream leisure tourist is not usually interested in towers. However, Manaca Iznaga Tower (about 7.5 miles northwest of Trinidad in Sancti Spiritus Province in the Valley of the Sugar Mills (Valle de los Ingenios) has an interesting history. At its peak, there were more than 50 mills and thousands of slaves worked the plantations throughout the valley. Cuba was the world's "sugar king" in the late 18th C and 19th C.

The tower was erected around 1816 and was the tallest structure in Cuba. Made with mud bricks and mortar, it stands 7 stories tall and its internal staircase has 184 steps. Manaca Iznaga Tower served a variety of purposes including being a means of surveilling/controlling slaves, detecting runaways, fires, and storms. The bell summoned people for daily prayers to the Virgin Mary in the morning, noon, and afternoon. It also was rung to signify the beginning and ending of the slaves' workday. In 1988, it was declared a World Heritage Site by UNESCO.

Fig 7.2 The Manaca Iznaga Tower

While Cuba has no dearth of atractions, economic

growth is down this year (2018 economic growth =

1% ; lower than last year because expected revenues from tourism, sugar, and mining were down). Tighter U.S. embargo controls are affecting tourism revenue and revenue from medical personnel/services Cuba provides abroad has declined (over 8,000 doctors from Brazil were recalled following the election of a far right president).

Fig 7.3 Valley of the Sugar Mills (Valle de los Ingenios)

Austerity measures to deal with slow growth include cuts in energy, fuel, and imported consumer goods. It is estimated that Cuba's import dependence is as much as 17 cents for every dollar of product produced and export revenues have declined each year since 2014. Aid from its chief ally, Venezuela, has declined because of that country's economic woes.

On a positive note, Cuba provides everyone relatively easy access to economic opportunities although the chances to grow beyond the subsistence level are sharply limited. For instance, Coco Cab (coconut taxi) a three-wheeled fiberglass shell that can travel at 30mph was introduced in late 1990s and is found commonly in Havana, Varadero, Trinidad. It is a great way for tourists to feel the air/ambience of the ride as they visit landmarks or destinations. While it makes for a fun memory of Cuba, it also provides a means of livelihood for thousands of Cuban youth.

Newly elected President Miguel Dias-Canel was welcomed by leaders of North Korea, Russia, China, etc. However, while they pledge solidarity, these countries are unlikely to make significant economic arrangements with Cuba because Cuba can't pay its bills and their patience is running out. Structural reforms are absolutely necessary to improve the Cuban economy.

Fig 7.4 A fish seller on his motor bike, by the streets of Havana

President Trump's National Security Adviser, John Bolton, has referred to Cuba, Venezuela, and Nicaragua as the "Troika of Tyranny" for causing immense human suffering and regional instability as it advocates communist tenets. The rapprochement of the Obama administration may be reduced by Trump if reforms aren't made such as eliminating the dual currency system by which the government pays meager wages to its workers, freeing its "political' prisoners, and improving human rights. The U.S. Embassy in Havana (established in March1953 and operated until January 1961; then, reopened recently) is currently undergoing drastic staff reduction due primarily to accusations of possible use of microwave weapons which caused dizziness, hearing loss, fatigue, insomnia, and other symptoms in staff members dating back to late 2016. Not a good sign for bilateral relations!

How about crimes in Cuba? Of course there is crime. Crime has existed in all societies throughout the centuries. However, there is a paucity of statistics on crime in Cuba because the government manufactures and controls the narrative. Since Castro's revolution, there is no private gun ownership and gun-related crimes are virtually non-existent. Why? Because the penalties for possessing and using a gun to commit a crime are so severe (possible life sentence). Murder rates are lower than in most countries throughout Latin America. While the death penalty still remains on the books for specific violent crimes, there have been no executions since 2003. Two of the primary minor crimes are currency exchange scams and pickpocketing. With virtually no organized gangs or drug activity, there are very few "no go zones" in Cuba.

We have a measured level of optimism about Cuba's destiny. We strongly believe Cuba has the potential to overcome its struggles. Regardless of one's political persuasion, the U.S.-Cuba relationship is a huge predictor of Cuba's success. Most Americans favor normalization of relations with Cuba as well as ending the embargo. It will be interesting to see what Diaz-Canel does. He talks of cautious change but always in the context of Cuban socialism. Among other changes, drafts of a new Cuban Constitution would grant greater recognition of private property, set age and term limits on some governmental positions (ex. presidents must be under 60 when first take office and can serve no more than two consecutive five year terms), and recognize marriage as being between two individuals rather than exclusively between a man and a woman. We earnestly hope these and other leadership initiatives coupled with changes in geopolitics would lead Cuba's surge to greater social and economic heights.

Further Reading

Bethell, L. (Ed.). (1993). *Cuba: a short history*. Cambridge University Press.

Cabezas, A. L. (2009). *Economies of desire: Sex and tourism in Cuba and the Dominican Republic*. Temple University Press.

Clancy, M. (2002). The globalization of sex tourism and Cuba: A commodity chains approach. *Studies in Comparative International Development, 36*(4), 63-88.

de Holan, P. M., & Phillips, N. (1997). Sun, sand, and hard currency: Tourism in Cuba. *Annals of Tourism Research, 24*(4), 777-795.

De la Fuente, A. (2001). *A nation for all: Race, inequality, and politics in twentieth-century Cuba*. Univ of North Carolina Press.

Dilla, H., & Oxhorn, P. (2002). The Virtues and Misfortunes of Civil Society in Cuba. *Latin American Perspectives, 29*(4), 11-30.

Eckstein, S. E. (2004). *Back from the future: Cuba under Castro*. Routledge.

Feinsilver, J. M. (1989). Cuba as a" world medical power": The politics of symbolism. *Latin American Research Review*, *24*(2), 1-34.

Feinsilver, J. M. (1989). Cuba as a" world medical power": The politics of symbolism. *Latin American Research Review*, *24*(2), 1-34.

Fernandez, N. (1999). Women, Race, and Tourism in Cuba. *Sun, Sex, and Gold: Tourism and Sex Work in the Caribbean. K. Kempadoo, ed*, 81-89.

Goodrich, J. N. (1993). Socialist Cuba: A study of health tourism. *Journal of Travel Research*, *32*(1), 36-41.

Gott, R. (2005). *Cuba: A new history*. Yale University Press.

Henthorne, T. L., & George, B. P. (2009). Transformation of Tourism Business in the Communist Cuba: A Critical Analysis. *International*

Journal of Business Insights & Transformation, 3(1), 8-26.

Henthorne, T. L., George, B. P., & Miller, M. M. (2016). Unique selling propositions and destination branding: A longitudinal perspective on the Caribbean tourism in transition. *Turizam: međunarodni znanstveno-stručni časopis*, 64(3), 261-275.

Hernandez-Reguant, A. (Ed.). (2009). *Cuba in the Special Period: Culture and Ideology in the 1990s*. Springer.

Herrera, A. O. R. (Ed.). (2012). *Cuba: idea of a nation displaced*. SUNY Press.

Jayawardena, C. (2003). Revolution to revolution: why is tourism booming in Cuba?. *International Journal of Contemporary Hospitality Management*, 15(1), 52-58.

LeoGrande, W. M., & Kornbluh, P. (2015). *Back channel to Cuba: The hidden history of negotiations between Washington and Havana*. UNC Press Books.

Miller, M. M., Henthorne, T. L., & George, B. P. (2008). The competitiveness of the Cuban tourism industry in the twenty-first century: A strategic re-evaluation. *Journal of Travel Research*, *46*(3), 268-278.

O'Connell Davidson, J. (1996). Sex tourism in Cuba. *Race & Class*, *38*(1), 39-48.

Padilla, A., & McElroy, J. L. (2007). Cuba and Caribbean tourism after Castro. *Annals of Tourism Research*, *34*(3), 649-672.

Romeu, R. (2008). *Vacation over: implications for the Caribbean of opening US-Cuba Tourism* (No. 8-162). International Monetary Fund.

Sanchez, P. M., & Adams, K. M. (2008). The Janus-faced character of tourism in Cuba. *Annals of tourism research*, *35*(1), 27-46.

Schwartz, R. (1999). *Pleasure island: Tourism and temptation in Cuba*. U of Nebraska Press.

Skwiot, C. (2011). *The purposes of paradise: US tourism and empire in Cuba and Hawai'i.* University of Pennsylvania Press.

Spencer, R. (2016). *Development tourism: lessons from Cuba.* Routledge.

Taylor Jr, H. L., & McGlynn, L. (2009). International tourism in Cuba: Can capitalism be used to save socialism? *Futures, 41*(6), 405-413.

West, A. (1997). *Tropics of History: Cuba Imagined.* Greenwood Publishing Group.

Wood, P., & Jayawardena, C. (2003). Cuba: hero of the Caribbean? A profile of its tourism education strategy. *International Journal of Contemporary Hospitality Management, 15*(3), 151-155.

About the Authors

 **Babu George**, PhD, DBA, is associate professor of management and the coordinator of international programs at Fort Hays State University, USA. He has been a visiting professor at various higher education institutions around the world. In the past, he has worked for Swiss Management Center University, University of Liverpool, Alaska Pacific University, and the University of Southern Mississippi, among others. Since 2001, Dr. George has been a consultant for destination management organizations in the Caribbean and elsewhere. He has led numerous tourism-focused research projects in the Caribbean region.

Thomas R Panko, PhD. A sociologist by training, has been a professor at the University of Southern Mississippi School of Criminal Justice for the past thirty-five years. He has made scholarly presentations in Russia, India, and Canada. He has also administered/taught on international educational programs in England, France and Jamaica. One of his current research interests is tourism in the Caribbean. His travels in Cuba have whetted his interest for further research on socio-economic and developmental issues affecting that country.

www.ingramcontent.com/pod-product-compliance
Lightning Source LLC
Chambersburg PA
CBHW071314220526
45468CB00001B/375